Arrivals and Departures

Nina Berkhout

BuschekBooks

Ottawa

Library and Archives Canada Cataloguing in Publication

Berkhout, Nina, 1975–
Arrivals and departures / Nina Berkhout.

Poems.
ISBN 978-1-894543-61-3

I. Title.

PS8553.E688A77 2010   C811'.6   C2010-901714-5

Cover image: Joyce Wieland, *Cooling Room II* (1964). Courtesy National Gallery of Canada. Photo © NGC

Epigraph: from *Duino Elegies* by Rainer Maria Rilke, (transl. John Waterfield: Edwin Mellen Press), used with permission.

Printed in Winnipeg, MB, Canada, by Hignell Book Printing.

BuschekBooks, P.O. Box 74053, 5 Beechwood Avenue
Ottawa, Ontario, Canada K1M 2H9
www.buschekbooks.com

BuschekBooks gratefully acknowledges the support of the Canada Council for the Arts for its publishing program.

Canada Council   **Conseil des Arts**
for the Arts   **du Canada**

Contents

To the memory of Jan Berkhout (1908 – 2009)
& Rie Kruiver Berkhout (1921 – 2010)

Who has not sat expectant
before the curtain of the heart's theatre?
And up it went. A scenery of farewells.

Rainer Maria Rilke

i Half-life

February.
The sky glows like polished bone.
It's not spring yet, far from it.
The groundhog has seen its shadow.

Everything is in place:
keys on the countertop,
a half-full bowl of ripened fruit—
rinds thick as oil paints—

bonsai on the sill, roots exposed
in a pot of gravel and moss.
The tree is dying.
What were we thinking in this climate?

With all your boxes gone,
I'm surrounded by light shafts
and silence.

Only the note is missing
from this still life you left me.

I'm looking for a palpable sign.
Tucked inside a jacket sleeve
or slipped between pages
of a book you know I'll reread.

In the kitchen cupboards
or in the garbage can:
in the smell of things,
in the most heightened of my senses.

When the phone rings,
hope gallops through me
as if I'd swallowed
the horizon's rising sun.
I'll pull the cord tomorrow.

All I wear is the rust sweater
I was knitting for you.
It has no sleeves and needs washing.

Oh, you'll feel bare awhile,
says my mother. Emptiness
lodges itself at the base
of my spine, a green pearl.

Smoke curls out
the bedroom's dormer window.

I occupy myself
by counting the number of times
my eyelids close and open,

working from the known
to the unknown,
top soil to bottom layers.

Add and remove blankets,
blinds down.
Extinguish the last cigarette.

In my dreams,
you barter your vital organs
at market stalls

until nothing remains of you
but a pelt that was the moon.

Mostly I'm not sleeping,
like the old who don't sleep,
their joints crammed with attics
and sharp-edged trunks,

shoulders afflicted by coffins,
heads stuffed with jingles.

Everyone says be grateful
for the years of picnics
and balloon festivals. I am.

Even now, when I think of you,
the pulse at my neck
and wrists and other areas
gently taps beneath my skin
like bound lobster claws in a tank.

Because of you I recognize
what strangers leave behind
in distant lands.

I know why plants
are short and yellow
over buried walls and tall
and green in ditches and pits.

I know that the age
of an object depends on
the level of soil it's found in.

I know that when an archaeologist
digs, nothing, no matter
how small, is missed.

In the bath, as if in a sand patch,
I groom water.
Smooth it into a grid of squares
with stakes and strings.

These sacred spaces you catalogue,
silted-in ports and docks,
submerged villages and prehistoric
camps—all endless affairs

sketched in grimy field books.
Nonetheless I'll wait in this pool
that's become unpleasantly chilly.
In case you transcribe me

into your margins again
like a ghost word created in error,
copied and recopied,
eventually entering language.

The spillage along fault lines,
the drillings and blasts
should have strengthened us

into arteries of turquoise minerals
pulsating within a quarry
or tulips photosynthesizing,
stalks growing long after stems

have been cut. Instead we resorted
to thoughtlessness, progressively
closing jar lids too tightly
for one another's reopening.

It's too bad we can't lay blame
on a catastrophic event.

The origin of earthquakes
doesn't explain
how we hit rock bottom,
our decline as gradual
as the erosion of mountains.

There's no pinpointing when
we ate wolf for dinner,
turned our backs in bed
and moved permanently
to a stony ravine.

I thieved your promises
like gold coins. Now I'm a crow
surrounded by shiny objects,

painting my nails fuchsia
so no one notices this ridge
of water between depressions,

this primeval body curled
into an arch, poised and in control
before shattering on shore.

Greater than a cruise liner,
my adoration for you.
What keeps a thing so enormous
and heavy from sinking?

Watch out he's a charmer
is the only advice my father gave.
We were watching a French film.

The jilted are always sewing
trinkets into their chests
in French films, he added. A lock
of hair, a ribbon. Such nonsense!

This I did not do,
preferring silver wire thread
through the ankles—pricey shackles
tarnishing in my veins.

White horses canter across the window.
I press my face against the pane
until my cheek melts them away,
burning a secret into their sad manes:
you were my solarium.

But drawers of tears
next to lavender sachets are useless.

You despise sentimentality;
conscientiously scraped it off us
with brushes and dental picks,
confiscating it, masked,
as a demolisher would asbestos.

It's going to take a lot more ice
to get through this.

If the ancients are right
and the liver is the seat of all passions
I'm killing this emotional disorder
one bottle at a time. Make no mistake,
I could sew a royal train
made entirely of brown paper bags.

Here you are again in the album
crouching down, dirt in the lungs,
retrieving nothing. How you feel
the weeks you dig and dig
and only find a shard
is how I feel most days lately.

The metal bit
embedded in my heel
doesn't bother me anymore.

Sometimes I look forward
to the sensation of stepping
into a momentary stinging.

Other times I tell myself,
today I'm not getting up
or, by the time he arrives,
the food will be cold.

Don't be sorry. I'm not alone.
A hyena sits across from me
at the table, wearing a silk ascot.

He offers posies
and laughter as I feed him
a smile and eat the buds.

Truth is a butter
he licks from his mangled paw
with a petal tongue.

Evenings, we dress up
for appointments to drown
in underwater forests.

Outside, snow angels
build momentum
for flight but this migraine
is an obstacle to soaring.

What I know of god's
attendant messengers recedes
behind me, a drifting feather.

Faith is a gleaming scripture
withdrawing from our sphere.

It mirrors my heart beat
and yours straight back
toward us in flashing attacks

of light

                what

                                pain,

one-sided
        and pulsating.

How much louder it is
when we scream inside our heads
than when we scream out loud.

My out loud scream lasts seconds
before I lose my breath
or my voice cracks.

Inside my head the scream goes on
clear as midnight mass, never ending.

You might as well
quit shoveling; human history
can't be understood
by what you exhume.

If you were near
I'd take you by the hand
and show you

the expanding crevice
in the hill behind the house
where stars retreat to expire.

I'd tell you all
about fractures in soil
no longer safe to walk on.

You reshelved our romance;
gave it the lifespan
of a clay tablet.

Some sanctuaries
are supposed to be protected,
one doesn't expect knives
beneath the library's floorboards
or poisoned pamphlets
in the stacks, this isn't the name
of the rose.

Of all the souvenirs
from your expeditions,
what's unfastening me
is this Russian nesting doll,

figure inside
wooden figure inside
figure inside figure clutching

pitchforks and roosters, then a baby
that doesn't open.

I have no reason for wounds.
I've sacrificed little for you.

In contrast to the suicide bomber,
it's not as if my existence
consisted of a leading up to us.

Our luck faltered, that's all.
Spun out of control
like the cyclist rouletting
around the velodrome.

It was only a question of time,
tilted on our steep oval track,
before we'd tip over.

What can the psychologist
of migrating geese
do for torn minds trailing
a vanishing frost line?

What can he do
for your settlement pattern,
the waiting for natural disasters,

excavating sites
until they're gone for good
then waiting for disaster again?

My words keep bleeding
off the page.

Like a widow I find myself
talking about you in the past-tense
to anyone who'll listen.

Interminable daylight stretches
beyond the firmament.
The sky is covered in gills.
I don't know where to send this.

Everything has an order.
Five years ago your eyes
crashed into me with more force
than a ship-breaking yard.

Five years later it's still winter.
My fingers are blue
and the buses have stopped running.

This week I read in the paper
that there isn't anything left to discover
in the Valley of the Kings.

The only birds in the yard
are waxwings, who flew in
with grand gestures when it was coldest.

The tablecloth is stained.
I have no other news.

ii Praha

You told me once
that the archaeological horizon
is what we'd observe

if we went back
to a specific point in time.

You took me places
with no written record;
gave me cities
lifted from paintings, the sea

a shimmering black caviar
spread around us.

If twilight would let me in,
I'd brighten Venus
and chain her to our balcony.

What crumbles in Prague
goes unnoticed.

The astronomical clock
repositions our planets;
splits calendars
in the old town square

till thorns in our longings
are reborn
into majestic piercing spires.

In the blue hour when flower
perfume is strongest,
you speak of lost civilizations
and remove my dress.

All the while my heart
is a butterfly zoo.

It hardly matters you know
but don't tell me
this will be our last holiday;

hardly matters
when you joke lovingly
that I'm your noble savage.

It could be the garnet ring
we contemplated in the antiquary.
It could simply be that the coffee
tastes better here. It could be your body
illuminating mine before we drop
soundlessly or it could be Kafka's tomb.

To shoot the beloved's profile
against a saint's or to embrace
the bridge tower's deceiving echoes—

the clichés luring us
to the Charles Bridge are the same
clichés that lure all lovers
to the Charles Bridge.

But all lovers don't
scout out the bridge at 4 a.m.
to witness the moment
when lanterns and city lights go out

and the river Vltava flows
so quietly, deep in its basin,
as if it had died.

Wherever we go we're taken
for newlyweds. Tenderness and pleasure
and mutual affection nip at our heels
like stray dogs.

Whenever you say my name,
the splendour of Prague is infinite
and whenever you gaze
at its alluring women

my sense of ownership
is as profound as a treasure map
on which I've spent my life savings;

gone into debt, then bankruptcy
without determining
the location of the valuable spell
that binds our devotion.

Your declarations pour through
the loudspeaker like a tonic
and I'm in awe of your wisdom.

In the lecture hall your audience
swarms around you, flies on sugar.

They haven't a clue
that what you unearth is a forgery;
that for every landscape you hack into,
a colony of spirits perishes.

Fables hide in narrow lanes of Josefov
and inside the marionette shop
when you say, yes, forever,
yes, string-pulling

me up the marble staircase
to our suite of plush furnishings
where moonlight filters in on cue
through lace curtains.

Your collarbone holds an imprint
of the earth's magnetic pole.

Nightly without fail, your lips
wipe freckles from my throat,
diamonds.

How confidently
you march away from the rooftop
terrace, blowing kisses.

My arm sails up at full mast
but my voice is a deserted cave
at the bottom of a cliff.

There goes my wayward Galahad
escorting his disciples to the grail,
conjuring jawbones
and skulls from imagination,

criss-crossing cobbled streets
where linens are flags of surrender
hanging listlessly on clotheslines.

Crystal breakfast tables scatter
around the lobby, dismantling me.

I've given myself bruises
walking into corners
because you're not here
to say careful, *careful*.

Minor dramas serving
as evidence—before the bread
and marmalade appear—
that this is real and not a hoax,
this is what couples *do*: they travel.

You're not by the statue
where we said we'd meet
tonight for evensong:
a ticket for the scrapbook.

The choral circle is a shining tiara
of hymns. In the pitch of bells
and air vibrations carrying foreign music,
I almost forget you aren't here

until I remember
and my concentration shifts to forgetting,
which causes me to forget my sister
on her birthday.

Surely this must be heaven's
laundromat. With the cunning
of fabric softener, arguments
and wrinkles elude our pockets
after a warm rinse cycle
at the foot of a guilty fountain.
All that's needed
are sweet-smelling chemicals
to help the iron glide,
and a suitcase of extra padding
for the next twelve months back home.

I'm in the way of my younger self
in Wenceslas Square.

Don't tell me you don't notice
their exotic accents and cigarillo legs
as they chirp around in bright costumes
like parrots in a pageant
competing for the same cage.

In my university years it was about memorizing
enclosed boundaries. But these clever birds!
Bonding themselves to you
so your jaw starts clenching during sleep.
As though you were inside Enlightenment. Torched.

At least when Prague fades,
a veiled fresco, we'll have this box
of candy glazed like the pastel buildings
and richly decorated, each bite
bringing a weakened sense of delight.

Strike anywhere,
these matches are foolproof

and there's something
to be said for drinking mimosas
at the bar that's a brilliant aquarium,

followed by a stroll
containing such intimacy
that by the time we reach the Tyn Church
all I can think of while you describe

a seventeenth-century fire
are children's names
and the wool required
for colourful handmade scarves.

The fog persists for days,
yet it hasn't rained since we arrived.
I almost wish it would.

To gloss the aspects of ourselves
we invent. And because the hope
I feel waking with you
implies an element of despair.

Rainfall would dissolve
this doom theme I keep dreaming.
And the trappings of elevators
creeping steadily downward.

What are we avoiding?
Faces concealed amongst gravestones
in the Jewish cemetery.

A bench without arm rests
outside the gate.

Not so much the bench
but the indirect crushing injury
of the bench's acute silence;

the places between our ribs
that we don't know what to do with
where light cuts through
our breathing in harsh stabs.

Imposing shade draws us to shrines
lacking adequate ventilation.
It's easy to lose sight of each other
in vast museums. If only we could plunder
this jubilee exhibition, gather courage
from the collection of weapons
used in periods of distress.

Really, why would anyone
be exempt from the curse of the golem
thriving in the synagogue's garret?

We should applaud his efforts
to alter our qualities and defects
with ritual incantations

but darling it's not working, his lyrics
aren't enough to summon
what's already inanimate inside.

You chose a pretty ending for us.

On a day of touring castles
your confession blossoms
from your perfect mouth:
a flower's dark center.

The only cloud above us
hoods the sun.

When did you grow tired
and half-empty of desire?

Not even the Bohemian countryside
can supply paramedics
for such an occasion, just fields
of poppies thriving in disturbed soil.

There comes a time
when even the bartender
is hostile. When, like corkscrews,
we twist in on ourselves and away
from each other, limping with resolve
all the way to the farewell banquet.

I'm delaying us in Prague.
Or were you ever even here
or am I chasing visions
in a silhouette or finger on the lens?

There was an old man in a nearby village
who made alabaster plates and bowls,
his atelier covered in a fine,
white powder. He barely exhaled

when he spoke. The stories he recounted
began with devastation
and focused on the aftermath.

While the terrain beneath us
shifted, he stood still.

iii Arrivals and Departures

I found the sign I was looking for
on the pillowcase.

The solid remains of a fire lie
in an ash strand of your hair,
it isn't logical.

You're Earth, I'm Water,
we should compliment one another
unless you're the property

water can't hydrate;
unless you're the night
when water gives up finding soil.

During our last year together,
I hated you so much my teeth hurt.

I remind myself how, toward the end,
we agreed on a single fact:
this city's greyness.

I remind myself
how we battled it out
with fluctuating temperatures:

snow melting, falling, melting
with slamming doors, the ground
exhausted, whispering *leave me covered.*

There were owls along the way
but we ignored them.
We both have dark eyes,
everyone knows
dark eyes are tougher to get through.

How many trowels
would it take to carve out the past?

There's a memory I can't amputate.
A throbbing phantom limb
refusing to part with my truncated soul:
Rice Lake one hot august afternoon,
our second summer together.

I painted you asleep in the grass.
As mosquitoes dried on the canvas
I remember thinking, in all likelihood,
you loved me less already.

I once ached to see the pyramids,
but I never got there.
With age, such yearnings
can be dissolved in kettles of vinegar.

Unfortunately
where we're concerned, illusions
are more difficult to eradicate,
like the swelling of a complicated tumor
or the unraveling of a hunter's tapestry
in which the solitary unicorn
is tortured.

Is it possible that spring's
calm breeze is carrying our prayers
across a remote tundra
on the backs of thousands of spiders
wafting delicately upwards
to a celestial grove of zero gravity
where nothing's trampled?

It's said that the recovery time
from a relationship
amounts to half the time
the relationship lasted.

For three months
I've notched your absence
inside my sleeve
like a student hiding crib notes
before the big exam.

Technically I have
twenty-six months to go.

I realize I won't die
when hunger returns

and all that's left in the fridge
is a bottle of gin and a container
of alfalfa sprouts, recalling a union

where we took and took and took
until things got messy
and we turned slimy, undiminished.

Looking for food reminds me
what was wasted
during one of our worst fights.

I filled your tan suede boot
with salsa, mustard, ink.
How we laughed when we made up.
It was hilarious at the time!

You washed the boot
and it came clean, a true miracle.
Then you asked if I'd kept
the other boot.

What friends are convincing me to do
is as unoriginal as your arrivals
and departures:

I've dyed my hair and cut bangs
to cover recent lines.
I'm taking vitamins and joining yoga,
pottery, a dance class.

I've scoured the house;
polished off your fingerprints
with magic erasers.

I could admit that without you
I'm the lead weight under the ocean floor,
forgotten with the wreck
but what's the point.

Like the tiered wedding cake,
in your domain it's inevitable
that newer structures be built
on top of old remnants.

As these drafts are a tiresome variation
of the same score, with clarity
I accept my flawed begging—
this metronomic repetition
in a city of incessant recycling.

I'm not equipped with binoculars.

Avoiding you
would have meant avoiding
the outdoors. High ground.
Open spaces.

The squirrels in the backyard
are the acrobats, not me.

What do you think of moving
your shadow ever so slightly off
my hips, over to the coffee table

to hide the burn in the carpet,
the vase placed just so?
It's for the best.

As the saying goes, anywhere
surveyors have been
there's nothing but dust afterwards.

Everything has an order.
It's too warm for blizzards now.

Even in needle park
the daffodils bloom,
it hasn't all gone to hell
like you thought it would.

All along we should have been
planting gardens.

All along we should have
soldiered on, whacking through
vines and mud, bouquets tall as rifles
in our knapsacks.

The mail slot brings no letters,
face plate noisy in the wind
or are those the shutters
of our dilapidated cottage?

I had lunar stories to send you
but the moon is cordoned off
with yellow tape;
she's sick and slowly eroding.

My therapist recommends crying.
Her fat happiness baffles me.
She knows little of genuine grief

or the investigation of fissures
on the concrete floor
in a warehouse of undeliverables.

What happens
when you stop wondering
whether you'll bump into your beloved
and even then (this is when
it should happen), you don't?

When it dawns on you—
in the middle of Spanish class
or spinning class or a rerun
of The Sopranos—

that you'll never see
each other again, you're living
continents apart
and you've both grown old?

We're all downstream
from someone else's drain,
repeating our errors
like loops in a fisherman's net
until the brave one swims away.

I was never brave.

These days, my love is unclaimed
luggage on a carousel,

going round and round
while in another airport I'm waiting
empty-handed.

Everyone left long ago,
not even gulls
spiralling against the sun are constant.

What can I do but watch
as you recede in the crowd
and pass through the gates,
forgetting to look back.

If only you'd turn around
once more if only you would turn
around you'd hear me
say goodbye.

Here it is

      the last

                of the snowballs,
maybe a pebble

      or two
inside, one for you one

for me

                    catch.

I miss
the goodness of you,
unmentioned in this
botched record;

your qualities
and how I pilfered them.

Quiet now.

For the requiem
of red heart pills laced
with magnificent ossuaries,

our joy beating wildly
up the glass staircase,
no cuts on our feet, treading
softly,
here we go.

Nina Berkhout grew up in Calgary. She has a degree in classical studies from the University of Calgary and an MA in museum studies from the University of Toronto. She is the author of the poetry collections *Letters from Deadman's Cay* (NeWest Press, 2003), *This Way the Road* (NeWest Press, 2005) and *Pas de Deux* (Turnstone Press, 2006). She currently lives in Ottawa and works at the National Gallery of Canada.